Ohio

Books in the Seeds of a Nation series include:

California

Florida

Illinois

Indiana

Minnesota

New York

Texas

Seeds of a Nation

Ohio

P. M. Boekhoff and Stuart A. Kallen

KidHaven Press, an imprint of Gale Group, Inc.

P.O. Box 289009, San Diego, CA 92198-9009

On cover: *The Signing of the Treaty of Greene Ville* by Howard Chandler Christy.

Library of Congress Cataloging-in-Publication Data

Boekhoff, P. M. (Patti Marlene), 1957–
     Ohio/by P. M. Boekhoff and Stuart A. Kallen.
        p. cm.—(Seeds of a nation)
     Includes bibliographical references (p.).
      ISBN 0-7377-0948-0 (hardcover : alk. paper)
      1. Ohio—History—To 1787—Juvenile literature. 2.
     Ohio—History—1787–1865—Juvenile literature. I. Kallen, Stuart A.,
     1955– II. Title. III. Series.
        F495 .B64 2002
        977.1—dc21

2001002246

Contents

Chapter One

The Shawnee

Ohio is a leading industrial, mining, and farming state in the Midwest region of the United States. It is bordered by Michigan and Lake Erie to the north, Pennsylvania to the east, West Virginia and Kentucky to the south, and Indiana to the west. Although Ohio is the thirty-fifth largest state in size, it has the seventh largest population of all states, with over 11 million people living there in 2000.

Today people from all over the world live in Ohio, but its original residents were Native Americans who lived in the region for more than fifteen thousand years. About three thousand years ago, Native Americans built large sculptures, platforms, and burial chambers called earth mounds. The platforms were shaped like pyramids with flat tops, upon which temples and forts were built.

The Shawnee

The Mound Builders created more than ten thousand giant earth mounds from clay and stone. The largest such mound in the entire United States is the Great Serpent Mound near Hillsboro, Ohio. It is 1,335 feet long (almost a quarter of a mile) and looks like a giant snake trying to swallow a huge egg. The Mound Builders sculpted a great variety of other shapes in the Ohio River Valley. Some are round or square; others are shaped like animals, leaves, cones, and pyramids.

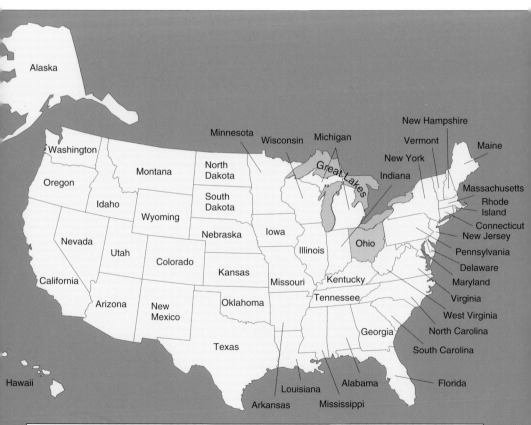

OHIO'S PLACE IN THE UNITED STATES TODAY

The Shawnee Tribe

Most of these earth mounds were built in the Scioto River Valley, near present-day Chillicothe, Ohio. For reasons unknown, the mound-building culture declined and disappeared. By the tenth century, the Chillicothe mound area was the central capital of the Shawnee tribe, whose ancestors were the ancient mound builders. Although no one is sure of their numbers, it is believed that about ten thousand Shawnee lived in the southern Ohio region.

Like many other Native American tribes, the Shawnee spoke their own version of a language known as Algonquian. Their name comes from the Algonquian word meaning "southerners." Shawnee people called themselves the Shawano, Shawnoe, or Shawanese.

Shawnee Women

From 900 to about 1650, the Shawnee lived in circular villages, near small rivers that flowed into the larger Ohio River. Women of the tribe built rectangular or circular houses out of poles that were covered with mats made of split cattails or bark. Their houses faced a central **plaza**, and for protection from enemies, the entire village was surrounded by a tall wooden fence. Each village had a large meetinghouse for **councils** and religious ceremonies.

In addition to building houses, Shawnee women performed other important work to help their families survive. Women farmed the fertile river valleys, growing corn, beans, squash, and sunflowers. They also gathered dozens of edible wild plants that grew in the thick forests.

Women were the doctors of the tribe, mixing medicine from herbs and setting broken bones. In addition, they made beautiful clay pottery, wove baskets, cooked and preserved food, and made clothing out of animal hides.

While women were in charge of the home, Shawnee men spent their days hunting and fishing. Men also spent a great deal of time preparing for war and fighting battles against enemy tribes with bows and arrows.

Circular houses built by Shawnee women faced a central plaza.

Shawnee women managed the home, while the men hunt-ed and fished for food.

The Beaver Wars

The bows and arrows of the Shawnee men were no match for the guns of the Iroquois warriors who came to Ohio around 1660. The Iroquois were a large group of powerful warriors from New York and Canada who were traditional enemies of the Shawnee and other Algonquian-speaking tribes.

The power of the Iroquois had been greatly increased by contact with European fur traders who began to visit the East Coast of America in the seventeenth century. These traders brought items such as cooking pots, cloth, knives, guns, alcohol, and other goods to the tribes. By trading beaver and other animal furs for these products, the Iroquois were among the first Native Americans to acquire guns.

After the Iroquois had captured and killed nearly all of the beaver in their region, they invaded homelands of other tribes to the west in order to search for more furs. These battles were waged from New York to the Mississippi River and were known as the Beaver Wars.

During the Beaver Wars, the Iroquois invaded Ohio. They swept through the Ohio River Valley and killed many Shawnee. The Iroquois, however, did not remain in the area. But they did clear the land of competing tribes so they could use the region as their own private hunting ground.

In the following years, the English offered to purchase the Ohio region from the Iroquois. The New York tribe agreed and took a wealth of trade goods in exchange for Shawnee land that they had no right to sell.

The Iroquois killed many Shawnee tribesmen while invading Ohio.

The Scattered Tribe

The surviving Ohio Shawnee broke up into five groups of a few thousand people. Some tribe members moved to Indiana; others went to Illinois, Pennsylvania, Maryland, the Carolinas, Georgia, Alabama, and Tennessee. Once a great thriving nation, the Shawnee were now homeless wanderers.

Despite their hardships, the Shawnee remained on friendly terms with other Algonquian-speaking tribes in the area. These tribes allowed the Shawnee to hunt on their land. In exchange for the hunting rights, the Shawnee helped prevent wars between tribes that were fighting over pieces of land. For instance, the Cherokee in Tennessee allowed several Shawnee bands to settle along their borders to protect them from their enemies, the Chickasaw.

After the Iroquois traded the Shawnee's rightful land to the English, the Shawnee, like those pictured here, became homeless wanderers.

Ohio

For fifty years the Shawnee wandered through mountains and prairies, creating new villages and then moving on. In this manner, the Shawnee acted as peacemakers and go-betweens for different cultures.

But the Iroquois continued to harass the Shawnee, capturing and killing them. Tribes that were friendly to the Shawnee also felt the wrath of the Iroquois. And it was a difficult time for most tribes in the region because the Beaver Wars had created many homeless, hungry **refugees**. Ancient borders between neighboring tribes were disturbed, and border conflicts increased between neighboring tribes.

Ohio was a favorite hunting ground for many tribes to visit, but it was unsafe to live there. The Iroquois destroyed any permanent settlements they could find. But small groups of Shawnee continued to visit Ohio to hunt. The Shawnee never lost their connection or surrendered their claim to their ancient homeland in the Ohio River Valley.

Chapter Two

People from Many Nations

B y the mid-1600s, most Native Americans who were native to Ohio had either died or left Ohio as a result of the Beaver Wars.

To add to their misery, European diseases such as smallpox and measles infected and killed thousands of Native Americans in every tribe throughout the region. The empty Ohio lands, rich in natural resources, soon attracted the attention of French fur traders in Canada.

In 1669 a hunter from the Iroquois tribe told French explorer René-Robert Cavelier, Sieur de La Salle, about a great river to the south. The Iroquois called it the Ohio, which means "beautiful river" in the Iroquois language.

European Exploration

Between 1669 and 1670, Cavelier and other French explorers entered Ohio from the north. During this time the French claimed all lands northwest of the

Ohio River, including present-day Ohio. The English also claimed to own Ohio, since the Iroquois had sold it to them in earlier years. And despite these other claims, the Iroquois traveled from their homeland in New York to hunt in Ohio and control the fur trade in the northern part of the region.

In the 1690s the Iroquois found that three tribes, the Shawnee, Delaware, and Miami, had moved back into southern Ohio along with dozens of French fur traders. The Iroquois attacked these people repeatedly but failed to drive them from the land.

Smallpox and measles, however, continued to weaken the tribes. By the 1700s diseases and Iroquois attacks had killed over half the Shawnee population.

Refugee Tribes

The surviving Shawnee settled in small scattered villages in southern Ohio. Meanwhile the power struggles over the fur trade between the English and French created many refugees from other tribes in the Great Lakes region. Some of these tribe members settled in northern Ohio.

The Wyandot, from present-day Ontario, Canada, were the first of these refugees. In the early 1700s they settled near Sandusky Bay and the Cuyahoga region, between Detroit and Cleveland. The Wyandot included survivors from the Huron, Tionantati, Erie, and Neutral tribes. After moving to Ohio, these tribes began to work in the English fur trade.

In the 1740s the Ottawa, a tribe from Canada and northern Michigan, settled in northwestern Ohio on

In the Iroquois language, Ohio means "beautiful river."

the edges of the Black Swamp. They had also been chased into the region by the Iroquois. The Ottawa were followed by the Mingo, who were friendly with the French and Shawnee.

By the 1740s about twenty-five hundred Wyandot, Mingo, and Ottawa had moved to northern Ohio. In southern Ohio small Shawnee hunting camps had turned into permanent villages. The Mingo began to settle among the Shawnee in the same villages. Soon the Delaware, from present-day Delaware and New

York, were also forced to flee their homeland and move in with the Shawnee in Ohio. By 1744 the Ohio Shawnee, Delaware, and Mingo lived in mixed villages with a combined population of ten thousand, including about two thousand warriors.

The French and Indian War

Despite the presence of thousands of Native Americans, British power continued to grow in the region as hundreds of English **colonists** from Virginia settled in Ohio to work in the fur trade. In 1747 businessmen in England and Virginia formed the Ohio Company to buy and settle the land. In 1749 the company sold 200,000 acres of the Ohio River Valley—actually owned by Native Americans—to colonists in Virginia. The next year the Ohio Company sent explorer Christopher Gist to map the Ohio country.

The French, however, were not about to surrender their fur trade in the Ohio Valley. Tensions increased between the English and French. In 1752 Charles Langlade, a French Indian, led two hundred French and Indian soldiers in a surprise raid on an English trading post in Ohio.

In 1754 the competition between the French and English fur trade exploded into the French and Indian War. In Ohio some Shawnee fought against the British, attacking frontiersmen who lived in their homeland. Other bands of Shawnee helped the British. The British won the war in 1763, and Ohio came under British rule.

Many English colonists from Virginia settled in Ohio to pursue the fur trade.

The British won the French and Indian War. A historical reenactment of the British in battle is pictured here.

Pontiac's Uprising

After winning the war, the British built a trading post at Fort Pitt just east of Ohio, in present-day Pittsburgh, Pennsylvania. With the French traders gone, the English began to treat the Native Americans as a conquered people, not as equal trading partners.

The French had provided annual gifts such as good blankets and ammunition to the Native Americans to help them survive during the cold winters. But the British only exchanged trade goods for animal pelts.

They refused to give annual gifts and often cheated the Native Americans or gave them less than the French had for the furs. These changes in trading practices caused great hardship among the tribes.

In 1763, the same year the British won the war, an Ottawa chief named Pontiac gathered warriors from many tribes to save his people from the British and reclaim their land. Under Pontiac's leadership, Shawnee, Delaware, and Mingo warriors captured Fort Pitt and killed six hundred Pennsylvania settlers. They also captured six other British forts in the Great Lakes region.

Shaken by the uprising, the British made peace with the Native Americans. They drew up the Royal **Proclamation** of 1763, reserving all lands west of the Allegheny Mountains, in New York and Pennsylvania, for the Native Americans. The

The great Ottawa chief, Pontiac, united many tribes to fight the British.

The Shawnee took many Europeans hostage during Pontiac's uprising.

Royal Proclamation helped keep peace until 1768, when the British ignored the proclamation and allowed thousands of white settlers to move into the Ohio region.

Relations between the Shawnee and the settlers were hostile. Tensions flared as frontiersmen sometimes shot Native Americans on sight. The Shawnee fought back and took European hostages. One such prisoner captured on June 5, 1771, was a seventeen-year-old German boy, Marmaduke van Swearingen, who was adopted by the Shawnee and renamed Blue Jacket. Van Swearingen learned the Shawnee language and eventually became a chief of the Mekoche band of the tribe. Blue Jacket would go on to become an important leader of his people. And in the coming years, Blue Jacket and the Shawnee would have to deal with a new enemy—American frontiersmen who would soon claim independence from British rule.

Chapter Three

The American Settlers

German missionaries from a Moravian Christian sect built the first European settlement in Ohio in 1772. They were aided by Native American converts from the Delaware tribe. The group built the town of Schoenbrunn (German for "beautiful spring") on the banks of the Tuscarawas and Muskingum Rivers near present-day New Philadelphia. The Moravians were pacifists, meaning they refused to fight in wars.

While the Moravian and Delaware people lived in peace, tensions were high between other tribes and English soldiers who lived in area forts. In 1774 the Virginia **militia,** under English command, attacked several Mingo and Shawnee villages, killing hundreds of Native American men, women, and children. Shawnee chief Cornstalk, realizing that he could not beat the English, asked for peace. As a result, Cornstalk signed a treaty with Virginia governor Lord Dunmore that opened tribal **territory** to English settlement.

The American Revolution

Between 1775 and 1783, American settlers fought for their independence from English rule in the American Revolution. Most of the Revolutionary War battles took place east of Ohio, but a huge wave of American settlers moved west to get away from the war. Fifty thousand American pioneers who lived in Pennsylvania, Virginia, and Kentucky moved to settle Ohio lands.

Ohio lay between the American military center at Fort Pitt, Pennsylvania and the British military center in Detroit, Michigan. Both sides recruited Native American warriors in Ohio to raid settlements in

American settlers fought for their independence from England in the Revolutionary War. A modern reenactment is pictured here.

Pennsylvania, Kentucky, and Virginia. The British and the Americans both offered trade goods and guns to warriors who would fight for their side. Shawnee leader Cornstalk supported the Americans, but it became impossible for him to control his aggressive young fighters, many of whom supported the British.

In 1777 Cornstalk traveled to Fort Randolph in Virginia to warn the Americans that his tribe was deeply divided in their loyalties. Instead of rewarding Cornstalk, the Americans put him in prison and then killed him. As a result of this betrayal, all the Native Americans in Ohio joined the British side except for the Christian Delaware, who remained neutral.

Fighting Continues

The new Shawnee leader, Chief Blackfish, became a bitter enemy of the Americans. Under Blackfish, the Shawnee raided and destroyed American villages in Virginia, Kentucky, and Pennsylvania, returning to their villages in Ohio with horses and other loot.

Americans struck back by burning down Ohio Shawnee villages and destroying their food supply. In 1779 American troops burned Old Chillicothe and killed Shawnee chief Blackfish. When they realized they were beaten, about four thousand Shawnee left the region and moved to Spanish-controlled Louisiana. Only about three thousand members of the Chillicothe and Mekoche tribes remained in Ohio. About 850 of those joined the English troops in raids on settlements in Kentucky.

In 1780 George Rogers Clark raised an American army of a thousand men and crossed the Ohio River to

Shawnee warriors prepare to raid an American settlement.

burn surviving Shawnee villages at the Battle of Piqua, near present-day Springfield, killing hundreds.

Signing Away the Land

In 1783 the Americans won the Revolutionary War and gained independence from English rule. The thirteen former British colonies in the East became the United States of America. The United States also claimed all land east of the Mississippi River and north of Florida, including Ohio. With this victory, the huge Ohio Territory was opened to American settlement.

In 1785, Congress sent George Rogers Clark (center) to meet with several tribes in an effort to get Native Americans to give up their land.

Americans surged into the West, but with the war over, much of the land was still controlled by Native Americans. In 1785 Congress sent George Rogers Clark to meet with four hundred Delaware, Wyandot, Ottawa, and Chippewa at Fort MacIntosh in Beaver, Pennsylvania. The Americans tried to force the tribes to give up their lands without delay.

Tribe members stubbornly refused to sign any treaties. To sway their opinion, the Americans fed them huge meals and gave them free alcohol for two weeks. On January 21, 1785, the tribe members, many of them very drunk, finally signed away a huge area of Ohio. The treaty confined the Delaware and Wyandot to the northeast corner of Ohio, opening the rest of the land to American settlement.

Shawnee leaders were not present at Fort MacIntosh. To obtain their land, American negotiators traveled to Shawnee territory and passed out whiskey to the young warriors while threatening the chiefs with a bloody war. On February 1, 1786, the Mekoche Shawnee signed a treaty that gave Americans their villages and hunting grounds east of the Miami River. The Chillicothe Shawnee, however, refused to sign the agreement and attacked settlers who flooded into Ohio after the treaties were signed.

The Northwest Territory

After the Revolutionary War, Thomas Jefferson, author of the Declaration of Independence, drafted the Northwest Ordinance, which went into effect in 1787.

Thomas Jefferson wrote the Northwest Ordinance, which created the region called the Northwest Territory.

The Northwest Ordinance created a region called the Northwest Territory, which included Ohio as well as present-day Indiana, Illinois, Michigan, Wisconsin, and part of Minnesota. The territory was ruled by Governor Arthur St. Clair, three judges, and a secretary. St. Clair was authorized to create laws and oversee land sales in the region. The ordinance stated that the territories would be divided into three to five states when the population of a given area reached sixty thousand.

Parts of Ohio were claimed by two eastern states, Connecticut and Virginia. To settle the land dispute, Congress gave Connecticut a section of northeast

Ohio called the Western Reserve, because it was reserved for the use of Connecticut citizens. Part of the Western Reserve, called the Firelands, was set aside for Connecticut citizens whose homes had been burned by the English during the American Revolution. Virginia was given a section of land between the Little Miami and Scioto Rivers in the southwest. It was called the Virginia Military District, reserved for Virginia war **veterans**.

In 1786 another group of war veterans formed the Ohio Company of Associates and bought 1.5 million acres of land in southeastern Ohio from the government. In 1788 they founded Marietta, where the Muskingum and Ohio Rivers meet.

Marietta was only the second large white settlement in Ohio since the Moravians arrived in 1772. In the years between, the region was the cause of great

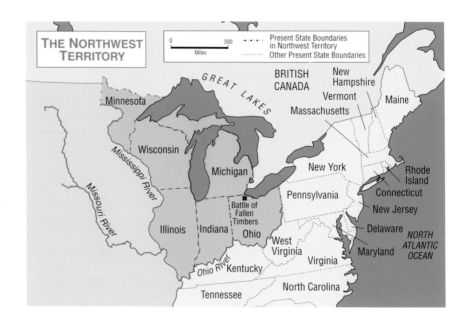

THE NORTHWEST TERRITORY

Present State Boundaries in Northwest Territory
Other Present State Boundaries

Congress gave part of the Western Reserve to Connecticut citizens. Another portion, pictured here, was given to Virginia and became the Virginia Military District.

dispute between Native Americans, British, and American settlers. Before peace would come to the region, however, several more bloody battles would have to be fought prior to Ohio becoming a state.

Chapter Four

The Seventeenth State

After the Northwest Ordinance, thousands of American settlers came from Kentucky and eastern states to settle in Ohio. They cut down trees to build log cabins and planted crops such as corn and wheat in the cleared fields.

Late in 1788 these settlers founded Losantiville, the third major white settlement in Ohio. Losantiville, later renamed Cincinnati, was made the capital of the Northwest Territory. In 1789 Fort Washington was built in Losantiville to protect the European settlers from Native Americans in the region who remained hostile to white settlement.

Americans launched three attacks on the tribes from Fort Washington. The first two, led by General Josiah Harmar in 1790 and Arthur St. Clair in 1791, were fought near the Ohio-Indiana border. Both were disastrous failures for the Americans. A Miami chief named Little Turtle had assembled warriors from many tribes and led them in successful **ambushes** against the Fort Washington troops.

Fallen Timbers

After these stinging defeats, American soldiers launched a third attack from Fort Washington, led by General "Mad" Anthony Wayne. Wayne's three thousand troops had been in training for nearly three years. These men built two outposts in Ohio, Fort Greenville and Fort Recovery.

Settlers on their way to Ohio navigate the Ohio River.

Little Turtle's warriors attacked Fort Recovery and found that Wayne's army was too strong to be defeated. The Miami chief advised his warriors to ask for a peace treaty, but some of the men wanted to fight on. In 1794 Blue Jacket assumed leadership of the tribes and made plans for war against Wayne.

The enemies met at Fallen Timbers near present-day Toledo, Ohio, on August 20, 1794. Wayne's army of three thousand attacked Blue Jacket's seven hundred warriors from the rear and defeated them in a bloody battle.

The Treaty of Greenville

After losing to Wayne at Fallen Timbers, Blue Jacket and ninety other chiefs met at Greenville, Ohio, to sign the Treaty of Greenville. This document gave American settlers about two-thirds of present-day Ohio. Native Americans were allowed to stay north and west of the treaty line, but the Americans could build forts in those regions. Blue Jacket was offered an honorary **commission** in the U.S. Army and a yearly salary. He accepted, ending his career as a leader of military resistance against the United States.

After the Treaty of Greenville, the Ohio Shawnee under Chief Black Hoof cooperated with the U.S. government and moved to northeastern Ohio to learn European farming methods. Within a few years, however, the government forced them to move out of Ohio. One Shawnee war chief named Tecumseh refused to leave and founded a village in Deer Creek, Ohio. There he gathered angry warriors from many tribes to unite and defend their culture, their land, and their people. But the power of the Native Americans of Ohio was broken. American settlers poured into the fertile river valleys of southern Ohio by the hundreds.

New Settlements

In the last few years of the 1700s, new settlements were founded all over Ohio. Cleveland was laid out in 1796

Shawnee chief Tecumseh (center) organized warriors from many tribes in an effort to protect their land and their heritage.

by Moses Cleaveland, one of the directors of the Connecticut Land Company. The same year Youngstown was founded by New Yorker John Young, who bought the township from the Connecticut Land Company. Also that year Virginians founded the village of Chillicothe near the site of the ancient Shawnee village on the west bank of the Scioto River. Once the site of Shawnee culture, Chillicothe was named the new capital of the Northwest Territory.

In 1798 Thomas Worthington, a wealthy land speculator, came to Ohio to build a mansion on a hill overlooking the Scioto River Valley just northwest of Chillicothe. As a member of the territorial legislature, Worthington began to work toward Ohio statehood.

The Seventeenth State

Before Ohio could become a state, the territory had to have at least five thousand people who were allowed to vote. To vote, a person had to be a white adult Christian male landowner. In 1797 Ohio took a census and found they would soon have enough qualified voters to become a state. This gave them the right to elect a legislature.

In 1799 Ohio's first house of representatives met in Cincinnati. William Henry Harrison was elected to represent the Ohio Territory in the U.S. Congress. Harrison pushed for Ohio statehood and made it easier for more Ohio settlers to own land and qualify to vote.

In 1800 Congress passed a law allowing Ohio to form a state government. In 1802 a convention met at Chillicothe to draft a state constitution. In 1803 Ohio

The skyscrapers of present-day Cleveland, Ohio, tower over the city.

had nearly seventy thousand white settlers, more than enough to qualify for statehood. President Thomas Jefferson signed the bill making Ohio the seventeenth state in the Union on March 1, 1803. Chillicothe became the first state capital. Edwin Tiffin became the first state governor, and Worthington became the state's first senator. In 1816 Columbus became Ohio's permanent state capital.

In its long history, Ohio was always a crossroads for Native American, and later European, traders. A cultural hub at the **strategic** center of the American heartland, Ohio has often played an important role in human affairs. From the ancient Native American mounds along the Ohio River to the modern skyscrapers of Cleveland, the people of Ohio have a long history of reaching for the sky.

Facts About Ohio

State capital: Columbus

State song: "Beautiful Ohio"

State motto: "With God, all things are possible."

State nicknames: Buckeye State, Mother of Presidents, Mother of Inventors

State tree: Ohio buckeye

State animal: white-tailed deer

State fish: walleye

State reptile: black racer snake

State bird: cardinal

State flower: scarlet carnation

State wildflower: trillium

State insect: ladybug

State fossil: trilobite

State gemstone: Ohio flint

Some Ohio wildlife: bass, beaver, blackbird, cardinal, catfish, chickadee, chipmunk, cowbird, coyote, deer, dove, duck, bald eagle, finch, fox, goose, groundhog, grouse, gull, hawk, heron, hummingbird, mink, mockingbird, muskrat, nuthatch, opossum, owl, perch, pheasant, pike, quail, rabbit, raccoon, skunk, sparrow, squirrel, starling, swallow, swan, thrush, turtle, vulture, weasel, whippoorwill, woodpecker, wren

Farm products: apples, sugar beets, celery, chickens, corn, cows, cucumbers, dairy products, eggs, grapes, hay, horses, mushrooms, oats, onions, peaches, pigs, popcorn, potatoes, rye, sheep, soybeans, strawberries, tobacco, tomatoes, wheat

Mining products: clay, coal, natural gas, gravel, gypsum, limestone, oil, peat, salt, sand, sandstone, shale

Manufactured products: books, magazines, newspapers, buses, cars, trucks, chemicals, electrical equipment, glass products, machinery, metal goods, paint, paper products, plastics, processed foods, rubber products, soap, tools, toys, wood products

Business and trade: communications, finance, insurance, printing and publishing, real estate, retail trade, tourism, transportation, wholesale trade

Famous people: Neil Armstrong, Erma Bombeck, Clarence Darrow, Doris Day, Phyllis Diller, Thomas Edison, Clark Gable, James A. Garfield, John Glenn, Ulysses S. Grant, Zane Grey, Arsenio Hall, Warren G. Harding, Benjamin Harrison, Rutherford B. Hayes, Maya Lin, William McKinley, Toni Morrison, Paul Newman, Annie Oakley, Pontiac, William Tecumseh Sherman, Steven Spielberg, Gloria Steinem, R. L. Stine, Carl Stokes, William H. Taft, Art Tatum, Tecumseh, James Thurber

Glossary

ambush: A sudden surprise attack from a hiding place.

colonist: A settler who lives in a land ruled by another country.

commission: The act of granting certain powers to carry out a task.

council: A group of people called together to talk about something.

militia: An army made up of ordinary citizens rather than soldiers.

plaza: A public square or open area in a town or city.

proclamation: An official public announcement.

refugee: One who runs away in search of help in times of war.

strategic: Important or necessary to a plan of action.

territory: An area of land under a certain government.

veteran: A person who has served in the armed forces.

For Further Exploration

Dennis Brindell Fradin, *From Sea to Shining Sea: Ohio.* Chicago: Childrens Press, 1993. Introduces the history, geography, industries, notable sights, and famous people of the Buckeye State.

Ann Heinrichs, *America the Beautiful: Ohio.* New York: Childrens Press, 1999. Describes the geography, plants, animals, history, economy, language, religions, culture, sports, art, and people of Ohio.

Janet Hubbard-Brown, *The Shawnee.* New York: Chelsea House, 1995. Presents an accurate portrayal of the history and culture of the Shawnee people.

Elaine Landau, *The Shawnee.* New York: Franklin Watts, 1997. Describes the history, culture, religion, and traditions of the Shawnee people.

Victoria Sherrow, *Celebrate the States: Ohio.* New York: Benchmark Books, 1999. Discusses the geographic features, history, government, people, and attractions of Ohio.

Index

Index

Picture Credits

About the Authors

P. M. Boekhoff is the author of several books on state history, art, and ecology, and a professional artist who has illustrated many book covers. In her spare time, she writes poetry and studies herbal medicine.

Stuart A. Kallen is the author of more than 150 non-fiction books for children and young adults. He has written extensively about Native Americans and American history. In addition, Mr. Kallen has written award-winning children's videos and television scripts. In his spare time, Kallen is a singer/songwriter/guitarist in San Diego, California.